Katharine Murphy
On Disruption

T0363065

hachette
AUSTRALIA

Every attempt has been made to locate the copyright holders for material quoted in this book. Any person or organisation that may have been overlooked or misattributed may contact the publisher.

Published in Australia and New Zealand in 2020
by Hachette Australia
(an imprint of Hachette Australia Pty Limited)
Level 17, 207 Kent Street, Sydney NSW 2000
www.hachette.com.au

First published in 2018 by Melbourne University Publishing

10 9 8 7 6 5 4 3 2 1

 A catalogue record for this book is available from the National Library of Australia

ISBN: 978 0 7336 4452 8 (paperback)

Original cover concept by Nada Backovic Design
Text design by Alice Graphics
Author photograph by Penny Bradfield
Typeset by Typeskill
Printed and bound in Australia by McPherson's Printing Group

The paper this book is printed on is certified against the Forest Stewardship Council® Standards. McPherson's Printing Group holds FSC® chain of custody certification SA-COC-005379. FSC® promotes environmentally responsible, socially beneficial and economically viable management of the world's forests.

To the memory of Michael Gordon, who lived this, taught me so much, and left us too soon.

It was the fag end of summer and I was decked out in a new linen three-piece suit from Sportscraft. I'm not sure why the suit seemed necessary, particularly one tailored for a generic 40-year-old professional woman when I was in my mid twenties, but I'd never been a journalist before. Did journalists wear suits? I'd only ever seen journalists socially, or talked to them on the phone. If they did suit up for the office, would it be power suits, or something more low-key in the suit range?

This was a point of anxiety, but I was intent on making a good impression. I knew I only had one shot.

In early February 1996, I sat at the Senate entrance of Parliament House waiting for one of my new colleagues to come downstairs and sign me in, my stomach full of butterflies. The costume masked my deep sense of inadequacy. I knew full well I'd talked myself into a job I wasn't at all qualified to do. 'Do not screw this up,' my hyper-alert brain said; an internal monologue, 'Shoulders back, chin up. Smile for Christ's sake.'

As soon as I entered the office the ludicrousness of the suit became clear. The Canberra bureau of the *Australian Financial Review* wasn't a place for suits outside of parliamentary sitting weeks. The drab cubicles overflowed with paper. Yellowing front pages were tacked on the walls. A couple of plants wilted in the windows. The people sitting inside the cubicles were not in suits.

My new colleagues looked at the suit and at me and then looked back at the suit. As kind as they were, I was as exposed as if I had walked into the office naked. I can still see the look on David Shires's face, the chief of staff; his polite attempt to hide his wry amusement from me until he swivelled his chair back around to his screen.

Before that day, I'd been a public servant. I'd finished university in 1991 and no one was landing their dream job in 1991. Your dream was to *get* a job. In the middle of a recession, opportunity seemed scarce.

I lucked out and got a graduate position in Canberra. I wore my mother's clothes for that interview because buying a suit was an extravagance beyond my meagre student means. I was interviewed for the Department of Industrial Relations by a woman who appeared deeply fascinated by the fact I wrote my honours thesis on Sylvia Plath. She felt, and said as much, that the department was chock full of economists and lawyers. Her view was the bureaucracy needed the odd alternative type.

Somehow, by sheer luck, as the designated alternative type, the kooky creative, I was packing a large bag for the train to Sydney and the overnight bus to Canberra. I had a farewell drink in my local pub with my friends and was berated by a friend-of-a-friend who had failed to get a graduate spot in either Treasury or the Department of Industrial Relations despite having a first-class honours degree in economics from Sydney University. 'How the fuck did you rank ahead of me?' was his not very cheery but not unreasonable bon voyage.

So it was fair to say the moment at the end of the summer of 1996 was not my first experience of being an impostor. But walking into political journalism, into one of the Canberra parliamentary press gallery's most high-performing bureaus, was a different experience from talking my way into the bureaucracy courtesy of a willing and broad-minded patron because I had no obvious career alternative.

Journalism was something I wanted to do and I couldn't quite believe it was beginning to happen.

The *Fin*'s affable bureau chief, Tom Burton, affectionately dubbed 'The Guru' by the young smart-arses of the office at that time, had taken me on after persistent prodding from a mutual friend of ours. Burton was comfortable with lateral hires, and so, fortunately, was the paper. Burton had worked inside the Canberra sausage factory before making the leap to journalism, and the paper's view was public servants were useful, because they were interested in policy and they understood how Canberra worked.

The *Fin* view of that time, or at least Burton's view as he expressed it to me, was people could be taught to write a news story, but it was harder to teach them how Canberra functioned, and it was harder for newcomers out of journalism school to build up the network of public service contacts I had already accumulated.

I arrived at the bureau during Paul Keating's last few weeks in the Lodge. The team was preparing for an election and me turning up in the middle of it mustn't have been that helpful. If my colleagues were resentful, they hid it well. The Guru thought bureaus worked best when they worked together. Unusually for a newspaper man, he was interested in managing people rather than letting headstrong rival correspondents slug it out in bursts of survival of the fittest. That inclusive disposition set the tone of the office. Various people, including Tom, kept me afloat over the few weeks we had before Keating materialised in the prime minister's courtyard to call the election.

There were a lot of joint by-lines, which really meant a lot of ghost writing, both in Canberra and in Sydney by news editor Pam Walkley, an experienced and highly efficient Scot, who had a habit of laughing as the daily deadlines crept closer. The more Pam laughed, the more she was under the pump. Pam's laugh was our daily barometer. Were we under control, or out of control?

When the 1996 election hit, the office emptied out. Reporters went with the leaders, on the wombat trail and out on the road to perform various assignments. Once election campaigns begin, the leaders execute a meticulously organised tour of marginal and targeted seats for the duration of the contest, and the Nationals leader hits the heartland—hence the wombat trail. The reporters travel along in the slipstream to ask questions, and soak up a sense of the psychology of the contest by watching the dispositions of the politicians and the people around them.

Given my cluelessness, I couldn't be let out on the road until towards the end of the campaign, and certainly not with the leaders, because back then the senior correspondents were deployed on the road with the two leaders, not the inexperienced new arrivals. Senior reporters travelled with the prime minister and the opposition leader because there was no live coverage broadcast back to Canberra to facilitate remote reporting. Dealing with the daily frontline coverage required experience.

It seemed safe to deploy me on a niche assignment, so I went to Launceston to interview Bob Brown, the Tasmanian Green, who was attempting to enter the Senate. The objective of the assignment was to write something interesting for the weekend. As it turned out I couldn't write anything remotely interesting, because I hadn't mastered the structure.

I wrote something terrible, which my colleague Michael Dwyer massaged into something less terrible. My embarrassment was overwhelming. Michael counselled against either panic or embarrassment, and just chiselled the copy expertly into shape. My colleagues all reassured me that the structure of news reports and long form was just formulaic. I would get it by plugging away, and then structure would become second nature. This reassurance prevented me dissolving into full tilt panic.

Election night rolled around and the office, minus the reporters deployed to the election night events with the two leaders, went out to the National Tally Room in Canberra to watch the results come in.

We packed provisions and watched as the John Howard landslide rolled in. There was plenty of time to mill about and talk to people, roaming around the green rooms behind the sets for the television networks covering the proceedings live, talking to the politicians coming off the broadcasts and the staff advising them.

There was time for us at the *Fin* to mill around because there was no requirement to file a word on election night. We didn't have a Sunday edition. There was no such thing as an online edition and no paper until Monday morning.

The size of the swing meant the result was clear from early in the night: out with Labor, in with the Coalition. A representative of the new Coalition government—it could have been Peter Costello, I can't remember—sent word of a brief press conference for the tally room reporters.

The Hawke and Keating governments had governed Australia for more than a decade, and their reformist zeal had transformed the country. That night in 1996 was the end of a very significant political era. A number of the reporters were processing the result slowly. Some were visibly in shock. I watched the reaction of the reporters as closely as the political protagonists, because I was trying to comprehend the enormity of a change of government in Canberra after a long period of stability. I was trying to read the cues around me.

When a government changes after four terms in office, a legacy is swept away, which is not only the sum of the decisions of political leaders, but all the blood, sweat and tears of reporters who have recorded the first draft of history.

Many of the reporters around me had learned to be journalists in this period. The Hawke and Keating governments had shaped their formative professional experiences, and their rhythms, styles and habits had become the sum of daily experience. When a government changes, a small universe explodes and is remade.

The journalists out in the tally room were used to the drama of Keating. Now John Howard was promising dullness as a virtue. Some of the women around me noted it was time to have children—after all, what would you miss if you had a few months off? Not much, apparently. Howard wanted us all to be comfortable and relaxed.

As the reporters gathered around the designated Coalition spokesman for the press conference, one started to cry, her tape recorder quivering in her hand.

She stood there, silently, with tears rolling down her cheeks, not moving, not pulling back. I was transfixed. Everyone else just ploughed on, heads down in notebooks, firing off questions.

I don't believe the tears were an expression of any partisan feeling; it looked like a human response to the knowledge that everything she'd known up until that point was about to change. More than a decade later, I didn't cry when John Howard lost office, but I remember the feeling I had watching his final National Press Club address, that a hole was opening in my universe. Something else was coming, a new chapter, a new tempo, a new story.

So in early March 1996, Canberra shifted on its axis as it does every time the government changes. Out in the National Tally Room, with our oversized whirring tape recorders, we were moving into the unknown.

As premonitions go, it was apposite. But truly, we had no idea.

I've begun this story at the start of my career in journalism, not because there is anything remarkable about me, or my experience, or about that particular moment in time, but because it situates us in a particular time and place.

We didn't know it then, but I'd arrived in journalism in the final decade of the print era. The craft I was intent on mastering in my opening period at the *Financial Review*, a specialised one, looked immutable—it was the dominant language of twentieth-century journalism. Print was its own kingdom. Print drove the news. But unbeknown to me, it was actually on its last legs.

Within the space of ten years, technological disruption would up-end our profession.

The change didn't arrive with an explosion. I can't mark any particular date in a calendar as being the critical day when all our certainties and habits would be revoked, but the last years of print played out over the life of that incoming Howard government. By the time Kevin Rudd and Labor swept into power in 2007, tipping Howard out of his own seat, we'd moved into a new paradigm.

The printing press was the technology that determined what sort of journalist I would be for the first ten years of my reporting life. Then, in my second decade in the Canberra press gallery, the internet required me to be something quite different.

The changes to the way journalists operate came in increments, little tidal surges. In telling this story, my own story, the story of my colleagues, I have the benefit of a divided career to help catalogue and explain what has changed, and try to assess some of the implications of that shift, both for us and for society. I can let you experience a profound change through my eyes in the hope it might explain some things.

To tell this story, let me first situate you in print.

The day of the print journalist for morning papers had a distinct tempo. Political reporters of my era would tune in to early morning radio news and current affairs bulletins, and read the papers cover to cover, before arriving at the office around mid-morning.

We would arrive mid-morning because there was little point in arriving any earlier.

There was no beast to feed. The deadlines were all in the evening, over several editions. We would file our material from about 7 p.m. onwards. Late breaking news could generally be handled until 10 or 11 p.m., and until midnight on the broadsheets.

The old print day was governed by two significant dimensions: time and space. Let's deal with time first. You had it. It was finite, and sometimes it felt much too finite, with nightly deadlines pressing on you like a weight, but you had empty space over every shift that required filling.

Our focus was not now, this instant, but tomorrow. The task was to look forward.

Our objective was to create the news of the next day. We would either break news and try to unearth a story yet to be written, or push the story of today forward with a new perspective, a new voice, a new insight.

Looking forward and breaking new ground requires legwork. You needed to get on the phone, get out of the office and grab people for coffee, lunch or dinner. The day was about hoovering up information, new facts, chasing fragments that might lead you to a whole sitting somewhere discreetly out of sight.

I'm labouring the point about time because it really was the essence of the exercise. That time between waking and filing was about gathering, both the material you needed for now, and the network you needed for tomorrow, and the next year, and the years after that. In Canberra that meant politicians, backroom staff, staff in the organisations of political parties; it meant public servants, agency heads and lobbyists who were helpful in following breadcrumb trails because they were in and out of the offices of principals, picking up their own impressions.

Space, the other significant dimension of the print universe, was finite too. The technology of the printing press, set to print a designated number of pages, created an in-built rationing system. There are only so many pages in a newspaper. Once we'd filled them, that was it.

The number of pages on any given day would wax and wane depending on advertising, and depending on how many pages had to be allocated across sections of the newspaper: news, sport, business, international, arts and culture. At the *Financial Review* there were lots of specialised sections that might need a page more than news, which was the home of our national political coverage.

A combination of the technology, the printing press and the business model, how many ads had been sold on any given day, set a hard limit on how much content would ever see the light of day. In print, we had to filter, sometimes aggressively, on big news days with only a limited number of news pages.

A lot happens in Canberra in any twenty-four hours. Much of it is new by definition, but not all of it is important. The in-built rationing of the print production cycle meant something had to be important if it was to be recorded for posterity twelve hours after it happened. It meant a lot of intraday material ended up on the cutting room floor rather than as the lead story on a news website, juiced up with a clickbait headline—but I'm getting ahead of myself.

The system wasn't perfect. A lot of crap and dross made it into newspapers, obviously, and we made mistakes. But it was harder to get flotsam into a newspaper when the dead-lines were fixed, space was finite, and the col-lective focus was on what we don't yet know rather than what someone foolishly said on a cable news channel or on social media that might generate a solid session of mid-after-noon clicks on a news website.

Another feature of my last print decade is also worth noting. Readers were very distant from journalists. By readers, I mean ordinary readers: people who read newspapers because they chose to, as opposed to the flotilla of stakeholders who needed to read them for professional reasons, and with whom journalists would have a lot of contact.

It was quite rare to meet ordinary readers. Some intrepid souls would get through to Canberra newspaper bureaus by phone, having tracked down the number. Some would succeed in speaking to reporters, but this wasn't that frequent.

We print types were reasonably invisible. Picture by-lines were a rarity, and we weren't yet on high rotation as pundits on television. No one in print, or at least no one I knew, spoke about the imperative of developing their personal brand as a journalist. Social media had not yet given us a communications channel to promote our work and reveal our own personality to readers.

In this period, for a print journalist, there was an element of being hidden in plain sight in the public square. We were the rumpled people behind the fashionably dressed television reporters, glimpsed every now and then behind a prime minister or a minister, pulling a face.

Unless you were very senior in the print hierarchy, the folks generally spoken of as doyens—a Michelle Grattan or a Paul Kelly—there was near anonymity and a physical distance from the audience. I remember going to the dentist when I'd been at the *Fin* for a few years to have my wisdom teeth extracted, and during the small talk before the sedation the dentist learned my profession. As an avid *Fin* reader he was delighted and exclaimed to the nurse, as if he'd discovered an exotic new species at large in the wild: 'This woman works at the *Financial Review*!'

As well as calling the bureau, readers made themselves known through letters to reporters—yes, letters, written out in long hand.

Sometimes correspondence brought praise, sometimes complaint. The feedback would also lag the work, coming in several days or even weeks after the fact. Generally praise came in neat copperplate and complaint in spidery script, or in strident capital letters. *Now look, girlie.*

Letters also made their way to the letters page of the paper. Generally the letters editor in head office would alert a reporter if some excoriating feedback was slated for publication the next day. That seems a quaint sort of courtesy now—that old-fashioned filtering and gatekeeping by head office telling you that Doris of Rose Bay was intent on correcting your poor grammar, or pointing out your terrible bias against that lovely John Howard—when the excoriation of journalists roils social media around the clock.

In the print era, readers were present but distant from the exercise. The social media revolution, which was to bring readers in closer proximity to journalism, was still a way off.

This was the daily rhythm of the print cycle; my milieu. The cycle obviously ran differently for print journalists back in the era when newspapers had morning and afternoon editions, when there were two or more editorial shifts, but that was over by the time I arrived.

The cycle has also, always, been different for news wire reporters and for radio journalists, with news reporters filing on the hour or half hour. Television also had deadlines through the day: morning and evening news bulletins, and then any late night updates.

I remember very early in my career watching the television reporters and the reporters in radio alley (which is what we called the group of offices housing the radio reporters in the Canberra press gallery) pump out hourly content with great skill and efficiency.

I was out at a press conference reasonably early in my reporting life with an ABC radio journalist. The event must have been very close to deadline, because the reporter walked out of the press conference, got on her enormous mobile phone, and filed an account of the event about two minutes after it concluded, aided by only a couple of notes on her pad.

I was transfixed by what for me was alien behaviour—the capacity to walk out of a live event and file immediately, with perfect accuracy, without breaking a sweat or missing a beat. How miraculous—filing on the spot, no time to think.

'How do you do that?' I asked her. 'I honestly don't think I could. How do you think that fast?'

She chuckled at the coddled print newbie. 'You just do it,' she said.

This might seem a bit eccentric, but I want to talk about cars.

When I talk to people outside my own profession about our decade of disruption, I've found that the following analogy cuts through and makes sense to people who aren't journalists.

The car analogy is also possibly psychic penance on my part. Like a lot of reporters of my vintage, I've written a bit over the years about structural adjustment in various industries. Many of us did, often glibly or righteously, at the *Financial Review*. We either ignored or muted the human dimension of the story because we were looking at disruption as an economic homily about what needed to happen to develop the open and flexible economy Bob Hawke and Paul Keating and John Howard said Australia needed.

Try to imagine yourself as a worker in a car factory who has assembled a car the same way, more or less, for about a decade, or significantly longer for the experienced hands. Sure, there were different models every now and then, perhaps requiring the assembly skills to be deployed at a more advanced level, but generally the requirement has been putting together a car using the same routine and tools.

Then imagine yourself waking up one morning, without any consultation or much foregrounding, and you wander into your entirely familiar workplace finding that all the machines have changed overnight. But that's not all; there are now new daily expectations about your productivity as well.

Imagine too there is a live audience sitting in front of you, all around you, so it feels like immersion—or a fish bowl, or theatre in the round—and your live audience are holding loud hailers, so they can call out feedback about your performance at will, with thoughts ranging from 'You stupid fat ugly bitch—call that a car?' to insightful and erudite observations that you find enormously helpful.

Bear in mind this kind of immersion has never happened before. Prior to this, visitors have sat mute beyond the factory gates, or been ushered through on a factory tour some distance from you. It feels pretty noisy, and you know you are exposed.

You feel particularly vulnerable because you are not carrying out business as usual here on the shop floor. Circumstances require that you get cracking on these new machines, with everyone watching, even though you aren't quite sure how they work, and what sort of car they will produce at the end of the day. You must because the boss has decreed this is the future, not because he or she necessarily wants it to be, but because it *is* the future, and we are powerless to argue with it.

If we all want to remain in the car manufacturing business, new developments in technology demand we adapt to innovative ways of vehicle assembly. We have to move much faster. You get going, desperately hoping you can fake this until you make it, and after a few shifts, over weeks and months, when the new pattern assumes a familiarity, you begin to think this might be okay. You feel like you can adjust to the weird, hyper-productive cacophony you work in, and it might even be fun.

You counsel yourself that lots of workers across the economy are facing similar pressures triggered by the same technological shift, and this serves you right in some cosmic sense.

But then the boss blows the whistle and gathers the entire assembly crew together. Sadly, there is more bad news. A great chunk of the workforce is about to be laid off, not because they've done anything wrong, but because the business doesn't sustain an enterprise on this scale.

Your panic at this development is exacerbated because it's clear very early that the people being paid to get off the production line are the old hands—the people who have been assembling cars for decades, and have the wisdom to figure out how to adapt to the new conditions while pulling off the confidence trick of convincing the shouting onlookers that nothing important has changed.

You have an epiphany. All of a sudden your future is very clear. The future is going to involve not only a shift in work practices—it is going to mean doing a lot more, with less.

You watch your friends, leaders and mentors pack up their workstations. Every day a new farewell email goes out from someone who shouldn't be going, signing off for good, and for a time you operate in a fog of grief and survivor guilt and confusion. You think maybe you should get out, too.

Given you all know my car analogy is actually about journalism, a brief diversion now into some facts and figures. In May 2017, the Media, Entertainment and Arts Alliance reported that 2500 Australian journalists have left the industry since 2011. That's about a quarter of the total number of journalists employed in Australia.

The New Beats project, a survey of journalist departures during or since 2012, funded by the Australian Research Council, says 1000 journalism jobs went in 2012 alone. The survey work suggests the average age of the departures is forty-nine, with the cohort of people taking redundancies averaging twenty-five years experience as working journalists.

Let's return to and persist with our car production analogy.

There are rounds of redundancies at the plant, one after another. The boss explains that people have to go because there's another problem. All businesses suffer cyclical downturns, but this downturn isn't cyclical. It's structural.

We can't recoup our production costs because consumers have now decided they don't want to pay for the new car we are currently assembling when it rolls off the production line.

They want their car for free, because early in this transformation process the car company thought it was a good idea to give away the early prototypes for free as a goodwill gesture, to build up a new generation of car consumers. Never mind that we'd previously requested payment for cars. Now people are used to getting cars for free. Sorry, guys, that's just the way things are now.

Just when you reach your tipping point on this factory floor, when you think you really can't do this—manage all this change and somehow be brave enough to ride out this uncertainty—the boss has a final piece of news.

The boss says we really aren't sure whether we will be able to keep control of the distribution of the cars we make anymore. A couple of new entrants, big global distribution giants, called Facebook, Google, Apple and Amazon, are using our cars and the cars made by the crew down the road to attract customers to their own businesses. These folks are now devouring the revenue that once came to us.

The online behemoths have, as Emily Bell, director of the Tow Center for Digital Journalism at Columbia's Graduate School of Journalism, put it succinctly in early 2016, 'cherry-picked the profitable parts of the publishing process and sidestepped the more expensive business of actually creating good journalism.'

There's one more hiccup. These new mass distributors don't want the responsibility of being carmakers, so they don't check the veracity of the products now washing through their system. Proliferating through their distribution channels are a whole lot of fake cars that look exactly like real cars, so understandably consumers can't always spot the difference. Now it's hard to know what is real and what isn't, further eroding our professional standing, and making our audience-in-the-round even more infuriated and alienated.

'But do carry on, folks,' your boss says to the stunned workforce. 'Buck up, we'll work something out.'

That's it.

That's what's happened to journalism in increments over the past decade, both here and around the world. Some of these trends have begun to shift or level out in more recent times, and some haven't.

I will come to specifics shortly, but first some general observations. Emily Bell is bang on when she notes our news ecosystem 'has changed more dramatically in the past five years than perhaps at any time in the past five hundred.'

In telling you this, my purpose is not to write a self-indulgent memoir of a golden age, now lost, or co-opt you in some epic lamentation on our behalf.

I really don't think our structural adjustment is more poignant than comparable stories playing out in other industries. What I'm chronicling here will be instantly recognisable to a lot of people in a lot of professions. The contingency created by technological disruption is one of the great, shared, anxieties of our age, and there is no end in sight, with robots gathering like a small army on the horizon. I don't think other workers somehow deserve to have their workflow upended but we journalists don't.

I do think we have to talk about what has happened with journalism, though, because I believe our disruption has a consequential impact on public discourse and on public life. What is happening to me and my colleagues affects you in ways that may not be obvious.

And while the great disruption dominates internal conversations within our own industry, and informs some of the better academic research going on in the journalism schools here and around the world, we aren't that good at being frank with our readers about the changes underway in our industry.

Culturally this is hard. We like to think of ourselves as hard-boiled characters. Reporters are our self-styled lions who would take a gunshot and file before going for medical treatment. The culture of journalism is 'Stop yapping, the show must go on.' Talking about our experiences is considered professionally self-indulgent. Why focus on our own travails when readers need us focused on our core mission—looking outward—rather than whining about ourselves?

There is some element of truth to this, of course. But I also suspect we don't talk about this as much as we should because there is an element of keeping up appearances, and preserving professional pride. We want our audiences close, but not that close, in case they give up on us. They might conclude this—journalism in 2018—is all a house of cards, and ours is an enterprise not worth supporting.

Persisting with straight talk, I also think that in my own sphere, which is political reporting, we sometimes prefer to hang a lantern over dysfunction in politics than interrogate the link between politics not functioning optimally and the disruption in our own industry.

There is an abundance of talk about crises in western democracies and it's a funny sort of coincidence that this alleged crisis in politics has coincided with a profound revolution in the media industry. These two developments are linked, and I suspect intimately so, but we journalists rarely admit it, and some of the scarifying commentary about the deficiencies of the political class reflects either a lack of journalistic self-reflection, or a deliberate deflection effort. Look. Over. There.

So now that my car production analogy is exhausted, let me run through some of the practical differences between the print and internet eras.

We've established I used to file several stories once a day, which would appear in a printed newspaper the next day.

These days, my deadline is now, or preferably five minutes ago. News is filed when it happens, not hours after the fact. The internet allows a plethora of live coverage, and audiences flock to it. In digital this means live blogs and constantly updated news stories on mainstream media websites, as well as off platform coverage, like live tweeting, or Facebook live. On television this means rolling news channels.

On my beat in Canberra, the change came in stages. I was working for *The Age* as one of the paper's dedicated political journalists when the big disruption happened. The internet bus hit us in the late 2000s. In a very short space of time, we went from producing *Age*-only content to producing content for the web, which would run across the Fairfax Media network.

In a matter of a year or two, we transformed from a print operation serving metropolitan broadsheets into a web-first news agency called Fairfax Media, with some of the daily copy, tweaked slightly, also landing in the paper the next day. We went from talking about print circulation to talking about building readership online, where a vast new audience beckoned.

Editors were focused on mining that new frontier, anticipating the finite horizon of print, developing content suitable for computers and tablets and smartphones. We were following consumers, who were looking for an immediate and mobile news experience.

A lot of us worried about the consequences: the risk of the daily coverage becoming generic, the risk of getting things wrong because we were producing stories so fast, a lack of diversity in an already concentrated media market in terms of ownership, and the inevitable job losses as coverage once deemed distinctive was now categorised as duplication.

We started out at Fairfax in the early transitional period with dedicated online reporters, generally more junior staff. However, as editors were motivated to chase the new mass audience online, with one of the big early metrics being 'reach', senior political staff were under pressure to file more through the day—news and commentary—because readers would be more likely to tune in to hear what we had to say.

Bit by bit, story by story, we sped up. We began filing all the time.

The implications of that for work intensification, I suspect, would be obvious to most people, but I can hover very briefly on one direct comparison that we might call a tale of two technological tempos. I began this story with the 1996 election, and the election night where I gathered information but did not file. By the election night of 2016, I filed live coverage in ten minute increments from an hour before the polls closed until midnight, then I recorded a podcast with colleagues, and wrote a piece that needed to run first up the next morning.

But so what? Sucks to be me, right? Tissue for my issue. Except work intensification is only part of this story, and in some ways, it's the least important part.

Something more profound happened than a bunch of people suddenly typing faster. It became clear early in the disruption that the internet news cycle had a different set of values to print; a different currency, if you like.

While print was about time (more of it) and space (less of it), the web was about time (less of it) and space (more or less unlimited).

While the rationing of print imposed some discipline of importance on the content for reasons I've already canvassed, the web loved new. Important still mattered. It wasn't junked. But it now had to sit alongside a new imperative, a new journalistic mission. Let's call that one: 'new, now'.

A new market opened up in intraday newsbreaks. Instead of print journalists looking with anxiety at the evening deadline, the race to publish was brought forward earlier in the day.

In practice, this meant stories that still could have used some development, some deliberation, were now getting a prominent run on news websites. Some of this work, particularly early in the transition, was half-baked. But there seemed little choice. It became harder to sit on material, to think about it, develop it, because of the risk your competitor would publish first, and without set deadlines, this could happen at any time, without warning.

You can see how this sudden redrawing of the boundaries, if unchecked by steady editorial leadership, could quickly devalue the currency of the 'scoop' from a Watergate-level investigation of many months to a decidedly flimsy intraday insight, badged 'exclusive'.

Sean Kelly, a former media adviser to Kevin Rudd and Julia Gillard and now a political commentator and writer, talks about the new content hunger driving a persistent sense of crisis in politics. He says the current disruption has created 'an absurdly high demand for content'.

'News has always been a business, no point pretending otherwise. And what do you do if you need to create more content with less money? You create cheap content,' Kelly says. 'What are the cheapest types of content to produce? Opinions and breaking news.

'The beauty of opinions is everyone's got one. The beauty of breaking news is that it doesn't have to be important, or even difficult to get: it just has to have happened in the recent past. So suddenly we've got opinions and breaking news everywhere.

'Breaking news has to be given a semblance of importance, so often, when we are talking about political news, it's presented as disastrous for a politician, when often it's nothing of the kind. And then, once the story has "broken", the talking heads or opinion writers are called in to give their view, and we are off to the races.'

What he's saying is the news cycle, courtesy of the technological shift, got a lot more breathless, and a lot more shouty.

During this period of change journalists faced choices. Stay, or go. Embrace digital, or try to ride it out somewhere in mildly ambivalent fashion.

I pushed forward. While I could see the problems, there were elements of the change I liked. I lobbied to do a daily live politics blog when parliament sat, in collaboration with a couple of talented photographers, because it seemed like that project could work. I was in for a penny, in for a pound.

I welcomed the redrawing of the boundary between journalist and audience.

While the downside of an audience that could talk back was obvious—'call that a car, you stupid fat, ugly, four-eyed bitch?'—I welcomed the fact that technology had forced journalists out of our smug little enclave. In fact, it abruptly ended the 'voice of God' era, where great men wrote the histories of other great men, and feigned omniscience with their readership. That insider conceit always seemed pompous and exclusionary to me, even before the internet made the fiction of journalist as Morgan Freeman-style God-narrator impossible to sustain.

I went forward with digital, largely because it was not a static form. It was dynamic, and fresh and interactive, and I was alive with possibilities. As we spun out of print and into the unknown, I felt all the feelings. Grief. Terror. Excitement. Hope. Despair. With the fervour of a convert, I used to bore the pants off the digital sceptics, convincing them that this would be a transition worth making.

It turns out we, the enthusiasts and the sceptics, were both right.

Disruption has produced a more dynamic and connected journalism for practitioners who have chosen to adapt to the new environment in that way. There are now myriad possibilities for storytelling provided you can deal with the work intensification and, somehow, remain on your feet, and maintain clarity; provided, of course, our employers can manage to remain solvent enough to pay journalists a living wage.

But technological disruption, and our professional response to it, has also produced a febrile, superficial, shouty, shallow, pugnacious cacophony of content, where sensation regularly trumps insight. Our institutional shouting as a profession now goes toe to toe with the take-no-prisoners culture of the internet, where bandwagons roll day and night, and where people gather in fractious enclaves hostile to alternative points of view.

At its worst, this cacophony looks and sounds and feels like end times. We should not mince words. At times the environment is not only destructive it is completely unbearable.

The proliferation of content and opinion over the past ten years has been truly mind-boggling. A friend in politics said to me recently he was of the view that the sheer volume of information now pulsing through the virtual public square was triggering instinctive human responses.

When deluged with competing 'facts', when institutions battled other institutions in public screaming matches about what is 'true', many people seemed inclined to fall back on their own instincts, or small 'p' prejudices. People were retreating to their own networks of trusted sources—like-minded friends, or organisations they'd self-selected as trustworthy, or media outlets that confirmed their own biases.

This trend, he felt, was supercharging the echo-chamber effect that makes public discourse often difficult to listen to.

Bernard Keane, *Crikey*'s political editor, also points to the psychological impacts of the internet, which is a broader societal phenomenon connected to the current disruption. 'We now remember differently to how we used to, because we have all existing information virtually at our fingertips.

'Our brains have been trained into a cue-reward cycle designed to keep us addicted to things like social media and apps, or, originally, email. We multitask a lot more. The peer-reviewed evidence is mixed, but I can't believe our capacity for deep concentration hasn't been curtailed—there are a lot of claims that it has but the neuroscience hasn't provided hard evidence yet.

'This is the most dramatic neurological change to humans since the advent of print technology—more important I think than the atomisation created by the mass media in the mid-twentieth century, but certainly on a par with that,' Keane says. 'The disruption isn't merely economic but psychological. We're an increasingly psychologically unmoored society.'

What is going on in the public square, one element of which is a decade of disruption in the media, would be of no consequence to anyone at all apart from us if this disruption had no impact beyond the borders of our own profession.

But the fact of the matter is our disruption is consequential to what happens in the public square.

Our disruption is society's disruption.

I've walked around the following question so many times, and had a version of its ensuing conversation with so many different colleagues, that I've now lost count. Did we, the disrupted media, somehow create Donald Trump?

Did we enable him? Did we allow him to slip past us, playing into the vacuum of the content-hungry cable news channels, dishing up the hourly soap opera they required, and relying on the alt-right ecosphere to applaud and amplify his nationalist message?

Commentator Waleed Aly is very much of this view. He and I thrashed this out with others at a social function towards the end of 2017. Later, I heard him share his thoughts on his ABC radio program *The Minefield*. 'Trump is not an aberration who offends media sensibilities. He's successful because he … obeys the logic of media,' Aly said. 'If you were trying to design a political candidate, a politician, to work in this age, then Donald Trump is very close to what you would get if you were doing it in a factory.'

Trump is endlessly entertaining, and immune to serious debate or analysis. He is the ideal leader for an environment where people don't pay attention to the serious, classical debates of politics. 'He is a candidate of spectacle,' Aly states.

Trump shows us that politics is now a mass culture exercise, which pitches democratic conversation into a different dimension. Aly fears a consequential rupture in public life, where there are now few, or no, rewards for serious discussion. 'If politics becomes a form of mass culture, I'm not sure what it's about.'

While Aly's thesis about Trump and what his election tells us about the state of politics in the digital age aligns with my own instinct—and I'd characterise it as correct enough to be chilling—in a way this is a typical journalists' way of seeing a problem.

We can situate our ecosystem at the centre of the known universe. We can forget that Trump is there, in the White House, fundamentally, because enough American voters in enough states put him there. Many of these voters will have consumed little or no mainstream media coverage, believing it is as unreliable as the empty promises of the protagonists.

If we take the 'we created Trump' thought to the nth degree, we can enter deeply silly territory. The media doesn't make things happen, or 'stop' things from happening. That's not our role.

If we believe the political media ecosystem defines the contours of the known universe—that it's the only reality—then we fall into the dangerous solipsism that journalists and their trenchant critics can easily fall into unless checked. Donald Trump launching a hostile takeover of the Republican Party and coming to office involves a more complex set of factors than the febrile mass media response to his rise.

But with all that acknowledged, we can't, and shouldn't, avoid a conversation about culpability. Professional self-awareness demands that we examine our own role in what is clearly a challenging time in many democracies, and that we understand we are not only reporting the story of contemporary politics, we are playing a role in shaping it.

Let me repeat that. We are part of the story. If things are bad, we need to interrogate ourselves as well as pointing the accusatory finger liberally at others.

To have the required level of self-awareness, we need to break away from one of our fixed points: a default view of ourselves as institutional value adders.

Journalists like to tell ourselves we make the world a better place by speaking truth to power. This is one of our foundational myths. Periodically, it is demonstrably true. Wrongdoing is exposed. Powerful people suffer consequences. But rather than putting *All the President's Men*, *The Post* or *Spotlight* on a loop and patting ourselves enthusiastically on the back, we need to reality check our own propaganda.

We need to own something difficult. We need to own the possibility that we are making things worse. We need to step inside that possibility, and let it settle on us, if we are to have any hope of living up to our professional ideals.

It is possible that after a decade of constant change, the media is collectively hollowed out, hyper-extended, and a bit untethered. It is also possible that we are burning ourselves and our audiences out in a relentless chase for the new—a minute-by-minute crusade that ultimately creates more heat than light, and plunges civic conversation into chaos and borderline unhinging.

Owning this possibility is a bit like base-jumping, or breaking the fourth wall—but we have no choice. If we are really truth seekers, and truth tellers, if we are the true servants of our audiences, rather than just mindlessly trying to shore up our place in the firmament, then we have to examine this possibility.

Right now, we can know this much: Trump has washed up in public life at the end of a disrupted media decade like an emphatic exclamation mark.

He's not the first faux outsider to arrive in politics to artfully capitalise on a crisis of institutional legitimacy, to mine the intense frustration of voters with establishment media and establishment politics. Given he's broken through from the fringe to centre stage, he's unlikely to be the last.

Given Trump-like politicians manifest in all democracies, we need to be conscious of two things.

We need to consider that politicians like Trump are good at playing us at our own game. We need to be aware that our professional obligation to cover the daily utterances of a political figure can manifest less as an institutional check—which is what we think it is—and more as straight out amplification. The choppy modern news cycle hands an open microphone to a politician like Trump.

The second thing we need to be attentive to is Trump's apparent capacity to sustain himself by heaping crisis on crisis. It seems counterintuitive—that a president somehow shores himself up in rolling chaos—but it seems to be happening.

This might change. It might all end in impeachment, resignation or recrimination, but at the time of writing, one breathless, shock-horror insight replaces the last one, and so it goes, with everything somehow equalling everything else, and everything gushing through like water shooting through a fire hose.

As Kyle Pope, the editor-in-chief and publisher of the *Columbia Journalism Review*, wrote in early 2018, 'I remain astonished by the ability of this former reality television star to be our assignment editor. He has a preternatural ability to intuit the bumps and swerves of the news cycle, enabling him to refocus attention on himself just as it is in danger of moving on.'

Pope notes the effect of this is that 'we are reading the same memes again and again, and the president, a savant at intuiting public sentiment, is doing everything he can to keep the treadmill moving.'

I suppose the organising question of the era might be: in this time of disruption, how do journalists cover a political leader who has risen to power in part by understanding, at an intuitive level, the new media norms—give me something new, now, preferably outrageous, preferably unscripted, preferably emotive, so an audience will read it and react and share—and by playing the media adroitly at its own game to sustain himself?

Watching the US media try to do their job and rise to the challenges of the Trump presidency is, honestly, like watching an extended session of *Catch-22*. Journalists have to watch the president and report. Watching powerful figures, and keeping them accountable, is the job.

That's our institutional role. We watch, we bear witness, and we report. It's important that we do that. That's how abuses of institutional power get prevented. The best of us possess the talent and the dogged persistence to be meticulously adversarial, to trip people up, in the public interest. Society needs that vigilance.

But when what you are watching is primarily dysfunction in various manifestations, and the presidential agenda you are tracking is stop-start at best, and either absent or incoherent at worst, the round-the-clock reporting will reflect that fundamental vacancy. Intrigues, if they are afoot, will dominate substance.

As frustration levels build, the daily record will become a ceaseless symphony of nothing, with the volume cranked up to eleven. The harmonic structure will be all dissonance, and no consonance, and that kind of symphony is hard to listen to. The natural human response is to disconnect, and disconnection and fatigue benefit the incumbent.

Thinking about Trump and his politics leads us inexorably to conflict, which is his one constant, and it is also a constant in media.

Conflict is not a new commodity in news. It's always been critical. One of my early journalistic mentors told me it wasn't really a news story unless there was conflict, and preferably the conflict needed to appear by the third paragraph.

But media disruption has intensified the conflict cycle, compressing it into smaller, louder, intraday bursts, and those constant interruptions have a material impact on political decision-making, both here and around the world.

Conflict is absolutely essential to the democratic process. It is a mechanism to settle contested points of view, or determine they can't be settled. The process of legislating is active conversation between competing worldviews, interests and ideologies—a kind of structural balancing.

But a couple of things are happening. The 'new, now' news cycle, where minute developments are reported in real time, means internal processes of consideration and decision-making as well as the external process of negotiation are disrupted much more frequently.

The disruptions then often materially impact outcomes—governments change course, drop ambitious ideas, shape shift to try to avoid an unmanageable stakeholder backlash.

Activism on social media also intervenes, and the combined effect is a ceaseless public commentary that now sits as an adjunct to policy making.

Martin Parkinson, the Secretary of the Department of the Prime Minister and Cabinet, reflected on this phenomenon in late 2017. He said the contemporary media cycle was focused on 'gotcha' moments and sensationalising routine internal government processes, which then had a ripple effect on internal deliberative procedures, stirring up rent seekers and what he politely termed 'stakeholders'.

'You begin to try and have a conversation with stakeholders about an issue and all of a sudden the social media campaigns are running either for or against the policy option,' Parkinson told Glyn Davis, the vice-chancellor of the University of Melbourne, on Davis's podcast *The Policy Shop*.

Parkinson says stakeholders now take definitive positions on policy before it is finalised, and the tempo has increased as a consequence, 'and that makes it much, much harder to do this sort of thoughtful, careful analysis and policy design that in the past we were able to do.'

The former Labor Cabinet minister Greg Combet expressed a similar view when I interviewed him in 2017 for a long-form piece about the toxic work environment of modern politics that was published in *Meanjin*. He lamented the absence of time to think, and reflect.

'With technology, and social media, the issues just move now with enormous dynamism,' Combet said. 'In years gone by, twenty or thirty years ago, issues could be considered more thoroughly. One issue could keep coming back to Cabinet on a regular basis. Now everything needs to be determined more efficiently. Things get easily reported in the media, you have to react to them. All of the circumstances mitigate against carefully considered long-term public policy.'

As well as the constant disruption to routine political deliberation, political conflict also appears to have entered a new phase.

In structural terms, conflict in a democracy is ultimately about synthesis and dispute settlement. It's a mechanism to achieve an outcome. But increasingly, conflict manifests in contemporary politics as a commodity or an end in itself. Prosecuting the war has become more important than negotiating the peace.

It's useful to step through this, bit by bit.

As Michael Wolff notes in *Fire and Fury*, his controversial fly-on-the-wall account of the Trump White House, politics is now immersed in the internet-driven culture of 'immediate response'—or what the media baron and former New York City mayor Michael Bloomberg has characterised as the 'instant referendum'.

Wolff talks about the Trump svengali Steve Bannon, who ran Breitbart, a right-wing 'news' website, before advising the presidential aspirant.

'Bannon's entire political career, such as it was, had been in political media. It was also in internet media—that is, the media ruled by immediate response,' Wolff says.

'The Breitbart formula was to so appal the liberals that the base was doubly satisfied, generating clicks in a ricochet of disgust and delight.

'You defined yourself by your enemy's reaction. Conflict was the media bait—hence now, the political churn. The new politics was not the art of the compromise, but the art of conflict.'

Politics as the art of conflict is not a phenomenon confined to the United States. In Australia, we had our own Trump precursor, Tony Abbott.

Abbott's government replaced the first minority government formed at the federal level in Australia since World War II. That hung parliament was characterised by deliberation and compromise, and by practical progress. Labor had to build coalitions for everything it wanted to implement, in two chambers. That parliament had a distinct deal-making milieu.

Abbott characterised this behaviour as aberrant, and illegitimate, and he styled himself as a crash-through figure, defined by strident rhetorical simplicity. Instead of Make America Great Again, and Drain the Swamp, we had Axe the Tax (which wasn't a tax, but never mind) and Stop the Boats—his own nationalist pitch.

Malcolm Turnbull has toned down Abbott's combativeness, and in the early phase of his prime ministership, he tried to create some public space for complex debate.

But his government also speaks out of both sides of its mouth. Turnbull likes to contrast his pragmatism with Abbott's obduracy, but he also persists with zero-sum rhetoric.

Turnbull faces significant internal pressure to muscle up against his Labor opponents, to be aggressive with product differentiation, and to play the man. As the public posturing appears not only ludicrously theatrical, but at times completely counterproductive to securing cross-parliamentary support for important public policy, I've asked government MPs to explain why they counsel in favour of ad hominem muscling up.

The answer is that public muscling up fires up the base. 'The base' in contemporary politics is a concept uttered in reverential tones. 'We must carry the base. We must not offend the base.'

But who is this base? In this country, with due respect to people in this category, the base is an unrepresentative sample of the Australian community—partisans, and partisans prepared to stick with voting for a major political party, fundraising for a major party, and volunteering in campaign efforts, at a time when the electoral trend is moving in exactly the opposite direction.

So the product differentiation we see in daily politics is not only manufactured conflict—partisans locked in studious dialogue and dog whistling with other partisans—but manufactured conflict carried out in a bubble, a kabuki play for a boutique audience, egged on by shock jocks and partisan bobble heads in the mainstream media, intent on their own narrowcasting exercise.

There is also that contemporary, tribal, zeitgeist dimension to conflict in the public square that Michael Wolff refers to in *Fire and Fury*—the Bannon objective of defining yourself by your enemy's reaction.

This is the politics of trolling. We see baiting like this playing out on both the right and the left.

As Wolff points out in the passage from his book I quoted earlier, conflict imperatives of contemporary mass media and politics are now fused.

Conflict has become a mechanism to rally a tribe—whether they are voters or audiences. A crude assertion of values, and framing your values as being in mortal conflict with the values of others, gives people distinct rallying places. If you know who your enemy is, then you know something of your own place in a cluttered and disorienting and hyper-connected world.

Tribalism has become a commodity, both for establishment politicians, who want to hold their core support against outsider insurgents, and for media companies, who need engaged audiences to survive the disruption that has played out brutally over the last ten years.

From where I sit, this looks like two sides of the same coin.

But where does this leave progress? If the objective is to make war and not peace, how does anything then get done?

There are some in contemporary politics who will tell you practical progress is overrated. I've had parliamentarians tell me voters aren't fixated on whether things in a legislative sense roll forwards or backwards, but they are interested in having their core beliefs reinforced by someone with a platform, or having someone in public life empathise with them and their view of the world.

This might sound cynical, even crushingly manipulative, the worst form of amoral backroom extemporising by some prepubescent amateur social scientist. But I discovered first-hand there was some basis to this perception during a field trip to South Australia in late 2016 to research a long-form piece on Nick Xenophon, the mercurial then crossbench South Australian senator in Canberra.

Over several days, in different contexts and locations, I spoke to a number of people who identified themselves as Xenophon voters—people of different ages and life experiences—who all said the same thing.

They supported Xenophon because he had a go, because he tried to do things differently. Whether he succeeded, or delivered, seemed completely beside the point.

It was really striking how these voters wanted an empathiser and an outsider, and that was the long and the short of their expectations.

I was seriously perturbed by it as a person who wants politics to change the world for the better. Establishment politicians are judged by an entirely different standard, whether you deliver or whether you don't—or perhaps not, perhaps things have fundamentally shifted.

Political leaders are periodically inclined to offer journalists counsel about how to respond to the disruptive pressures we now face. Julia Gillard thought the solution was don't write crap. 'Can't be that hard,' she noted in a famous homily at the National Press Club during the height of the carbon 'tax' hysteria.

Tony Abbott thought the media needed to censor intrigue, or at least anonymous intrigue; presumably, front-stabbing was in a different category. 'A febrile media culture has developed that rewards treachery,' Abbott said at his final media conference as prime minister. 'If there's one piece of advice I can give to the media, it's this: refuse to print self-serving claims that the person making them won't put his or her name to,' he said.

'Refuse to connive at dishonour by acting as the assassin's knife.'

Malcolm Turnbull has a habit of offering private homilies to the media at his annual Christmas drinks, empathising with our considerable commercial challenges, summoning our better angels with flattery about our important role in the ecosystem. Our country needs us not to be adrenalin-charged lunatics, jumping at every shadow—that sort of thing. Please.

Trump just dishes up circus. As Michael Wolff notes, the constant, daily, often more than once a day, pile-up of events, 'each cancelling out the one before, is the true aberration and novelty of the Trump presidency'—which is unfolding in the fashion of binge watching a television show. Just like a downloaded binge-watched Netflix drama, technology brings it to us, blow by blow.

Wolff also notes, tellingly, and with considerable insight, that it might just be the central tragedy of the news media that 'its old fashioned and even benighted civic-minded belief that politics is the highest form of news has helped transform it from a mass business to a narrowcast one.'

In other words, we are all chasing one another through a wormhole.

It's too soon to say how this story ends.

Nobody knows how this story ends.

Wondering, abstractly, about how all this might end is actually jumping way ahead of ourselves. Right now, media companies are preoccupied with survival, and our collective pathway to survival resides in the loyalty of our audiences.

Every morning at *Guardian Australia*, where I am currently political editor, our news conference opens with a question: how are the readers? The first item of business each day is a report on the readership over the past 24 hours. In addition to a read-out on the traffic stats, the engagement editor also provides an update about attention times, which is a measure of the span of time readers spend with any particular piece.

Reporters are given these readership breakdowns in a daily email circulated to staff in what I suspect is now standard industry practice. Similar traffic reports were also circulated to reporters when I worked at Fairfax.

I'm one of those people fascinated by analytics. When I was a live blogger, I routinely logged on to our in-house analytics tool to watch the readership stats in real time, and to observe how the blog was being shared on social media sites.

This behaviour might seem odd, or distracting, but I was curious to know what was happening. My curiosity is also risk free in this sense: I'm lucky to serve a benign employer who conceptualises analytics as a pathway to producing quality work. The house preoccupation is not clickbait, or virality, but how to maximise eyeballs for work we regard as important.

But even if you are, like me, fortunate enough to work for a quality-focused media organisation, and face zero pressure from editors to write for the clicks, this data, once it begins to settle on you, can still be a form of psychological tyranny.

It can change your mindset. It can create a new form of performative pressure that mimics the 'please like me' relentlessness of social media culture. Like social media, where likes are the crude metrics of personal acceptance and affirmation that can form little grappling hooks in your brain, readership analytics can be addictive.

While I'm old enough and stubborn enough not to define or value myself by my metrics, I know I want to be read, particularly when I've put a lot of thought into a column, or pursued a new idea, or broken a story.

When I've worked hard on a contribution and it's not that widely read, I interrogate myself as a direct consequence of the trove of knowledge I now have direct access to. How did that not work? How could I have made that more accessible? Why did scores of people read my incremental news story and only a handful that piece I spent days working up?

These were questions we print types never asked ourselves before the invention of readership analytics, because we didn't have any relevant reference points to prompt the self-assessment.

A newspaper was the sum of collective effort, not a cult of individual performance. It wouldn't have occurred to me to ponder whether anyone bought the paper because I had an interesting story on page one, or because Michelle Grattan had a regular column on Friday, except in the most abstract of ways.

Technology now allows us to map the habits of our audience in minute detail, and in doing so, we have created yardsticks for journalistic performance capable of influencing not only how we feel about ourselves as people and professionals, but also what we write and how we present information to the audience.

This is important and useful information to have, which is why we gather it, but it doesn't take much imagination to see how this knowledge can both be a force for good and also a motorway to the lowest common denominator.

To some degree, what you see on news websites is a direct reflection of your own news consumption habits. I think it's important to note that as media organisations begin to settle into the web era, which has now entered its second decade, we are seeing less churn, a bit more steadiness and a bit less frenzy. While generalisations are unhelpful, I think collectively, we are trying to steady ourselves and find a better balance between the new and the important. This consolidation phase we are entering now is critical.

But pap and crap continues to grab eyeballs, and will go on being produced by news sites chasing mass readership as long as a willing audience keeps clicking on the content. (Hint, hint. Change the world. Vote with your online reading habits. It will make a difference.)

By now, you will have gleaned there is a lot of pressure in the new media world, both on owners and editorial leaders, and on individuals. For individual journalists, pressure presents on multiple fronts. We are saturated in content, so much so that it dulls the senses. Plugging in some days can make me feel physically ill, because I know constant input drains my capacity for original thought. It makes everything feel dull, repetitive and derivative.

If you are a practitioner who cares about the future of the industry, there are also feelings of personal responsibility about the performance of your own content, because engaging content means an engaged audience, which is what every news organisation in the world is striving for.

The *Buzzfeed* journalist Mark Di Stefano, in an engaging diary of the 2016 election campaign that vividly captures the pressure-cooker environment most journalists now work in, spoke of one 'mild freak out' he experienced during that period, triggered by an email from his boss asking about traffic, and an email from a publisher about a book deadline.

'My face went red. I got so hot I had to take my jumper off. I thought I was having an anxiety attack. I ripped out my headphones, grabbed my wallet and walked outside,' Di Stefano says in *What a Time to Be Alive*. 'This wasn't going to plan—our reporting, this book, the campaign, it was crashing down on top of me and I couldn't breathe.'

I've not had an experience like that, but I do worry about burning out. I remember during that same election period having such an acute feeling of pent-up stress and physical containment that was only relieved by walking as quickly as possible up a hillside in my Canberra neighbourhood and then standing in the full blast of freezing winter air as the sun slowly sank in the west.

There was no specific trigger for it. No one chastised me, or pressured me, or demanded something from me. I'm actually surrounded by support. I'd just spent too long pounding out the ten-minute updates. I was massively overstimulated. Any sound felt like nails dragging down a chalkboard. My head felt like it was about to explode. I can still feel the sting on my face as I stood there, on the hilltop, in the bitter wind, for as long as it took for my head to clear, with the sun sinking, framed between a couple of eucalypts, and darkness pooling around me.

The pressure individuals feel is a manifestation of the collective pressure the industry faces as we seek to fortify our defences, and charge on through the uncertainty. Once newspapers could rely on a combination of a proprietor's support and a cover price and advertising revenue to bankroll their journalistic operations, but the internet has smashed our business model. So journalism has entered new territory; relationship territory.

We ask the 'how are the readers?' question, and news organisations everywhere ask their own variant of that same question, because we now need our audiences to be engaged with our journalistic mission. This is more than a bit of feel-good, a bit of touchy-feely, it is at the core of widespread experimentation going on in media companies trying to fathom and unpick the relationship between the audience and the work.

The current editorial and commercial objective is community building. As Steve Coll wrote in *The New Yorker* late in 2017: 'Amid the cacophony of the digital era, publishers and advertisers prize readers who are deeply engaged, not just clicking around sites. News organisations as distinct as [*The New York*] *Times* and Breitbart now think of their audiences as communities in formation, bound by common values.'

Like most everything about this period of disruption, there is upside and downside in active community building.

It's mostly upside. I like to know there are people out there who value truth seeking, and who support the efforts of journalists to keep powerful figures accountable. I'm also aware that our audiences comprise people who have information and valid expert perspectives to share, whether positive or critical, often more expert than my own. I like to hope that periodically I can deliver something useful to them, given that's why I'm a journalist.

But as someone concerned about the destructive impacts of hyper-polarisation and tribalism, I worry about how engaged media communities then define themselves, and interact with other engaged media communities.

One of the most noxious elements of the web, which was supposed to usher in a more democratic and liberal culture of free ideas and diffuse connections, is the shrieking hostility. The great open platform of the World Wide Web can be more accurately categorised as surly enclaves of niche narrowcasting, where the only agreeable content is content that confirms pre-existing biases.

I encounter people every day, both right-leaning and left-leaning, who are deeply hostile to information that doesn't reinforce their worldview, and when I say hostile, I mean hostile. Visceral. Unyielding and often abusive.

If you hang out online for any length of time, you will encounter this intolerance for alternative views. It's hard to miss. In the market you can see a proliferation of media operations intent on giving a niche audience precisely what it wants rather than expanding anyone's horizon, or posing an alternative view.

The combat culture of the web and social media incentivises this narrowcasting. If you can create a gated community for a digital 'news' service online, or for a subscription television channel, you can monetise it. Advertisers know who they are selling to, and it's clear some people are willing to pay if someone is kind enough to reinforce their prejudices.

Given this culture exists, and there are already people in the market intent on reinforcing it as a pathway to profits or influence, what of media organisations intent on carrying out old-school journalism—prioritising truth telling and verification above bias reinforcement and activism? Is there a cultural appetite for that? Will audiences be content with that, or could they demand something else?

If you put these trends together, you can see that deep audience engagement potentially triggers issues of editorial independence—a new manifestation of the oldest fight in journalism.

Someone has always owned commercial journalism. Often the someone has been a proprietor who likes wielding influence, and editors have had to walk the line between keeping the boss happy and serving the public interest. If audiences are the new owners, and have easy means of making their views known, it's possible this cycle will repeat itself in a new form.

By sounding this note of caution, it is not my intention to portray the current commercial strategies of major media companies around the world as some act of gross stupidity or some kind of sinister plot to carve up the world into advertising-friendly demographics. I don't think it's that at all. Mostly, community building is just intuitive. It is where digital logically takes you. The best news organisations around the world are also insisting they will hold true to the core journalistic value of pluralism as they seek to build communities of interest, which is encouraging for journalists who didn't sign up to be an undisclosed activist, a tribalist or a brand ambassador.

I've never run a news operation, or been on the commercial side of journalism, but as a practitioner, the community-building element of digital is obvious. When the internet cut a swathe through my own newsroom during the late 2000s, I carried around a campfire motif in my head to explain to seriously depressed people why I was choosing to be optimistic about a change that was wreaking havoc in my organisation.

Perhaps this was a coping mechanism. Perhaps I was just a serious prat. But whatever the truth of that, digital for me as a practitioner meant mediated intimacy with an audience. By this I mean you can build a community in digital in a more immediate and tactile way than you could build a community in print.

To explain this I need to take you back to my live politics blog project, which is the specific campfire I built. I thought the live blog could become a campfire for a particular community—a community of politics tragics—and in the daily coming together, oral history could be shared. I could report events as they happened, illustrated with pictures and video, I could talk with readers in comments threads and on social media, and include their observations in the project. So I, and others, built, and the readers came, and then the live blogs proliferated in this country—more campfires on more hillsides, animated and engaged communities of interest, swelling post by post.

If people value what you do, if they accept the sincerity of your premise, and your work ethic, and your desire to create a community with them, they might be persuaded to support you in your journalistic mission. This was my logic. I thought it was possible to renew the community mandate with that basic philosophy underpinning the effort. I very much hope it is.

Despite all the stress, saturation and uncertainty, this is a fascinating period of experimentation for media companies. While community building is the common objective, the methodologies and models to monetise an engaged readership are different. At the *Guardian*, our content remains open, and we have a membership program. Our readers, bless them, have rallied to the cause. In our parent company, revenue from readers now outstrips revenue from other sources.

Other media organisations are locking down the content to drive subscriptions. Some lock it down completely. Others are pursuing soft paywalls that provide a taste of the daily offering before forcing the consumer to commit.

In 2017, a fascinating special report about the future of journalism was published in *The Economist*. It detailed the 'funnels' created by soft paywalls to bring in paying customers. According to the report, Mark Thompson, the chief executive of *The New York Times*, had as his main preoccupation tweaking the 'geometry of the funnel' to shift more people away from their free access to a paid subscription.

Analytics track whether readers return to a particular columnist or to some other content, and they analyse the habits of readers just before their decision to sign up. This is what I mean about the work underway behind the scenes to map the relationship between readers and content.

In the US, there is much positive talk about the so-called Trump bump—the bump in subscriptions triggered since he took the presidency.

Stressed-out people might be tempted to hope. But Raju Narisetti, former senior vice-president, strategy, for News Corporation and now the chief executive of Gizmodo Media Group, sounds a necessary note of caution about what he calls the 'subscriptions syndrome'.

In a piece for the Nieman Lab, Narisetti notes that a number of US media outlets gained a lot of paying subscribers in 2017, and the headline numbers are 'impressive'. But he reasons that before we start thinking we've turned a collective corner, people need to consider where the subscriptions are coming from, and the average revenue per new subscriber.

He says media companies are not disclosing the costs of acquiring new subscribers, and it is not clear whether the subscribers will stick once they have to renew. 'We read a lot about the great subscription upside of the

"Trump Bump" in 2017,' Narisetti says. 'Now is the time to start asking about churn, please. Because pouring more into leaking buckets won't solve the existential business model challenges of any media company, however wishful our politics might want that to be.'

How do we make sense of any of this? What is journalism in these disrupted times, and how can we make it meaningful?

There is no way to know if the disruption will start to settle into a new normal, or whether chaos is the new normal. I sometimes wonder what will happen when the last of the print generation passes into history and the media landscape becomes populated solely by journalists and editors who have only known the ecosystem of the web, and have only experienced governments trying to govern in those choppy conditions.

I worry what will happen when no one remembers the more orderly times of the past, when those times actually pass into memoir and collective lore, because right now those times are still proximate enough to remember, and to inform the values and experiences of the present.

Will it matter, the true passing of that era, or is remembering that past immaterial, just a fleeting indulgence?

Certain things can be known. I do know that good journalism still matters, and it's critically important to fight for its survival. I know that finding the truth and telling it still matters. I know that readers can sense when someone is doing an honest day's work, and when they are not.

I can tell you without any shadow of a doubt what I think good journalism is, and to help me do that, I'm going to borrow the principles that Bill Kovach and Tom Rosenstiel laid down in their book, *The Elements of Journalism*.

Good journalism involves a steadfast commitment to the truth. There is a belief that citizens come first. There is a commitment to the discipline of verification, which is different from being neutral, or objective, which no one is, given we are all humans—this means your truth-seeking methodology as a journalist is fact- and evidence-based.

Journalism has to be independent, and vigilant. As the authors note, it means 'watching over the powerful few in society on behalf of the many to guard against tyranny'. Good journalism should canvass a diversity of views, striving to keep coverage proportionate rather than sensational (truth, guys; it's important), and it should also allow practitioners to exercise their conscience in a professional sense.

These are solid principles, in any era.

To distil all of that down, I believe journalism is about truth.

But I also know it can be hard, sometimes, to establish what is true, and what isn't. Journalists only ever pick up fragments of the whole. What we don't know generally dwarfs what we can be certain about, and we have to filter competing versions of the same history, which is a kind of scientific method, but sometimes a frustratingly inexact one.

Over the summer I've written this book, there has been a lively debate about the Michael Wolff account of the Trump White House in *Fire and Fury*, which I've cited approvingly a couple of times.

Wolff is a contentious journalistic figure, regarded by some of his critics as an unreliable narrator. There's been some handwringing in media circles about the stupendous irony of an unreliable narrator recounting the 'truest' (and by that, read cut-through) version of the Trump White House so far, produced—yet the author is quick to own the fact he's not entirely certain truth is the commodity he's delivered, given the protagonists are themselves unreliable narrators of their own histories.

While that thought strands us all in intellectual quicksand, this is the essential quicksand of journalism—or at least the kind of journalism I practise, the journalism of doubt, of grey areas, of contestability.

It is productive to own these difficulties, these shades and nuances, rather than pretend they don't exist, and produce screeds of righteous certainty, which are very easy to read, but are often intellectually dishonest. It's important to respect the audience enough to be transparent rather than write fiction dressed up as journalism.

The difficulties associated with identifying truth take us back to Bill Kovach and Tom Rosenstiel and the discipline of verification. It's a helpful way of thinking about journalistic truth seeking that allows a certain transcendence of the old debate about objectivity that has persisted in the profession for as long as I've been in it.

It's something of a fashion now to argue that journalists should just declare their biases and worldviews rather than adopting a traditional, buttoned-up, 'he said, she said' 'objectivity' construct.

The American journalism academic Jay Rosen is in this camp. 'This is the biggest shift, and the hardest for traditionalists to accept,' Rosen argues on his blog *PressThink*. 'It will probably take the longest to unfold. Drop the voice of the god, ditch the view from nowhere, and instead tell us where you're coming from. Then we can apply whatever discount rate we want.'

I've got a few issues with Rosen's line of reasoning. The first is I think readers can already guess where journalists are coming from, particularly if they write both news and commentary. We are all now so prolific it's hard to imagine what is being held back.

Regular readers of mine, or people who follow me on social media, or watch me on *Insiders* or *The Drum* or *Sky News*, would be able to supply a broad picture of my underlying values as a human being without me having to make a formal declaration. I reckon most fair-minded people would say Katharine Murphy is socially progressive, centrist economically, moderately obsessed with the health of the planet, and a bit mouthy. They'd be right.

I'm entirely sanguine about the specific disclosure Rosen suggests. I'd do that any day of the week. I could add several other disclosures if required: helicopter mum, wife-in-need-of-a-wife, cat fancier, wine drinker, plant assassin, the only person in the world who hasn't read *The Da Vinci Code*.

I also think Rosen is right about false balance being the mortal enemy of journalism—that 'he said, she said' construct where two unequal arguments are given equal weight. If you feel the need to balance the ledger just to tick a box somewhere, you are not a journalist. Frankly, you are an idiot.

But I depart from his central reasoning when he suggests audiences will trust journalists more if we tell them where we are coming from. I don't think that's right. I think audiences will trust us more if they know where we are coming from and they also know we are capable of suspending predispositions in the service of the truth.

I suspect this latter idea might need a little bit of unpacking.

For me, it's not enough just to give readers a declaration that I hold certain values. If I am a true servant of my audience, I should not trumpet my values in self-indulgent fashion, but instead need to follow the evidence, even if the evidence sometimes clashes with my own resting predispositions about a particular issue. This, for me, is the difference between a journalist and a partisan, or a theologian, or an ideologue.

I suspect readers like to know that journalists have principles, and those principles mean something, and are not sacrificed on the altar of ambition. Principles reassure, and buttress the professional effort, informing the activism that good journalism requires. Prejudices don't. Prejudices disrupt clear sight.

The thing I like most about verification is the self-abnegation it requires. It's a structural check on journalistic ego. For me, following the facts to the truth, or at least to a coherent landing point proximate to truth, is both a vital mental discipline and the acid test of whether you are committed to serving a cause larger than yourself.

If you are constantly in the road of your own inquiry, if you are tripping over yourself and your crusades on the path to enlightenment, lulled by the comfort that all is well because you've disclosed your biases to your audience, then you are automatically obscuring your view.

Now, for the big question—our collective future in the media. I am full of uncertainty. I brim with it. It's what drives me. It's my professional heartbeat.

I don't know if journalism will ultimately survive the great disruption, I don't know if I can sustain myself as a journalist through this period of change or whether I will burn out or be tossed out or go crazy.

Every day I mourn our losses, the mentors who are now living their lives beyond journalism, and I worry that we are the problem, not the solution, and I wonder how on earth this history will ultimately be written.

But rather than worrying ourselves to paralysis, my colleagues and I press on, trying to understand, and explain. We work very hard. We hope. We try to navigate the cross-currents. We try to serve as river guides in white water, and will go on doing that for as long as the endeavour remains viable.

In the end, it doesn't matter if we can't know the future. As the great biographer and diarist James Boswell, a river guide of his own era, noted breezily in *The Life of Samuel Johnson*, 'It matters not how a man dies, but how he lives. The act of dying is not of importance, it lasts so short a time.'

Acknowledgements

On Disruption is a collective work. Particular thanks to Lenore Taylor, Gabrielle Chan and the *Guardian* crew, and to Kath Viner, who is a beacon of journalistic purpose in challenging times. Thanks to Bernard Keane, Sean Kelly and Waleed Aly for specific contributions and thoughts, to Matthew Ricketson and Jonathan Green for offering me different ways to contribute, and to politicians who won't appreciate being outed but have listened patiently to me droning on. Thanks to Louise Adler and Sally Heath for insisting I could do this. Thanks most of all to Mark, Evie, Tom and Evan, who encourage and sustain me in this crazy vocation.